The L Words

Lust, Love, and Life

Conrod Thomas

Order this book online at www.trafford.com
or email orders@trafford.com

Most Trafford titles are also available at major online book retailers.

Printed in the United States of America.

ISBN: 978-1-4669-6017-6 (sc)
ISBN: 978-1-4669-6018-3 (hc)
ISBN: 978-1-4669-6019-0 (e)

Library of Congress Control Number: 2012917684

Trafford rev. 10/31/2012

www.trafford.com

North America & international
toll-free: 1 888 232 4444 (USA & Canada)
phone: 250 383 6864 • fax: 812 355 4082

Contents

Chapter 1
Lust

Chapter 2
Love

Chapter 3
Life

Chapter 1

Lust

Dedication

This is for the fathers, uncles, men who are not afraid of self expression, and who seeks understanding from self doubts, love, and meaning for their emotions, lust, freedom, and self esteem.

Sex Tones

I'm thinking about sex tones.
The type that heats up your body
And make you moan. The one that
Love you from your hip to
To your inner bones.
Sex tones.
Vibrate, rotate
And ejaculate. Run down
Your back and round to
Your belly and rubbing on your
Pussy.
Sex tones.
Feeling, sliding, and pounding
The bones,
Sex tones.
Creeping through your flesh
Grabbing on your breast,
Sex tones.
Tasting your wet Lips,
Licking your tongue and
Sucking the tip and swallow it down,
Sex tones.

Tempted to touch

Images ran ramped through my mind
When I saw you smile while looking at me.
I knew just enough to know
that my thoughts should just remain so.
I could not resist moving closer;
I could not resist telling you what it will be,
Couldn't resist making thoughts reality.
From expressing the way I've seen you walk,
The way your body express your tights,
The way your hair flow,
And the way these images move me.
I know that this desire should be left alone.
I know that there is something
That's similar in the way I feel,
And I know if I touched you once,
You would be tempted to let my hand stay,
Tempted to feel what's flowing through me,
So it can flow through you,
To express,
Explore,
Define,
And shape these images
Of temptations that we share.

Turn you on

Let me touch you;
and run my fingers behind your neck ever so; lightly.
Let me touch your shoulder,
and move the palm of my hand down
the center of your back; slowly.
Let me touch you,
with my lips, on your cheek,
and kiss you all over; softly
Let me touch you,
with my tongue,
and lick the tips of your breast;
repeatedly.
Let me hold your hand,
and place them on my chest.
Let me hold your body,
and press it firmly against mine.
Let me hold your legs,
bend you over,
and wrap them around my waist.
Let me hold your heart,
and cherish it forever.
Let our fingers touch,
and spark with passion.
Let our lips touch,
and suck with desire.
Let our hearts touch,
and beat together.
Let our souls touch,
and live as one.

Eye Candy

Slender
Flowing
Curves
Simply
Beautiful.
Elegance with every move
And softness with every touch
A look desired
And energy craved
A thing
Securely placed
Within a window to stare
While shining brightly
To assure attention.
A lovely crafted affection
A deeply moved perfection
A dream placed before you
A greatness above you
A calling
Pulling
Changing
Accepting.

Class Act

Easy target
Pick and go
Set the trap
And step back
Watch as the approach
Goes into effect
Timely moves
Glanced at a silhouette
Perfectly executed
Smooth and accurate
Each point played
And each point met
Beautiful dance
Of yours and mine
An obvious attraction
Set by destination
A well played plan
Elegance in motion

Men's Intuition

There's not much mystery to you
First though is how you can change this brother to fit,
You.
But you can't change innate character
And you get played.
Now a brother is a dog
Because you couldn't accept him as is.
And his innate instinct is to treat you like a bitch.
His intuition felt out, and if you were right,
There'd be no fuss at night, or at all.
Every minute would be grand
But,
His attitude did not go along
To your simple little plan
And his intuition
Picked you out from the start
Because the first view is usually true
And you, like all the other girls,
Tend to do what you do,
Best;
Try to change a bother.
And by the time you realized
It was too late
Because intuition held true,
And he had to do
What he had to do
Too.

Can't Be Touched

I be the one you can't see
Visible but can't touch
Realistic yet fantastic
If you wish
Take a lick
Satisfy your epidermis with this
Chocolate brown sugar cup with
Coconut milk eyes
Now you realize
You're between my sheets
Just one of those things that grows with time
I'll make you mine
No need to slow down or rewind
No other was made this fine
With the skills to amplify your most intimate desire
No you're not asleep
Tell me I'm sweet
Feel me reach deep
Now you realize
I'm visible but can't be touched
I'm your sugar cup
Come take a sip
Come a take a sup

Don't Touch

His breath flows over her body without a single touch to
her hairs which stands at attention from anticipating the
emotions driven by the thoughts of him and her alone.

His face move to hers and his lips move to her lips
Then stop short of kissing as her lips raises to touch his,
Leaving only puffed pulsating lips that felt the
heat of his breath that's eager to warm her
tongue with his, but he doesn't touch her.

He covers her body with a silk sheet and slowly passes
a feather over her from toes to her neck using only the
tip then follows through exhaling hot air from his lips
to her breast, belly, neck, and thighs without touching
her soft, inviting moist skin that begs to be touched,
But still, he doesn't touch her.

Hold

Grab the back
Force your lips together
Feel me push
Feel me pull
Racing through your legs
Everything
Hold on
Feel the flow
Anticipate the burst
Hold on
Feel the dick running in
Anticipate the tremors it bring
Lip clench, teeth begins to bite
Legs firm
Pressed on my hips
And move back
As I move forward
Hitting that cat
Giving that pussy
Hard
Passionate
Thrusts
In her
To hold

Sex

So confusing
Yet we strive to perfection
With our hips gyrations
Keeping the flow,
Smooth.
Intertwine,
Is love and lust
Which we cannot get away from,
As we breathe
Heavily
Or not, compared to what you've got,
And how to use it.
Sex
Give me some
Doesn't have to be perfect
But it will still be worth it
Cause if it didn't work for you
It still worked for me
With room to displace my affection
Is she the right one?
Well,
Sometimes it just doesn't matter
Except for the motion
The timing
The laying it down just right
Then the next night to follow
Maybe a little sooner,
Sex,
Full of confusion.

Touch

Touch
And it runs deep from your hyper senses
To your inner soul.
Touched
And felt tingles of electrical signals
Rush to your brain and through your body
Touch
And to feel that not so subtle connection
Touched
To release the tension within
Touch
To tease the soul
Touched
To improve the connection

Plumb

A sexual touch
A feeling
A rush
No hands
Just lust
A rise
In temperature
Glands open
No words spoken
A look
A sigh
A force
Moving out
Legs weak
Souls meet
Less sleep
Thoughts sweet
Lust
Must touch
Must feel
Blood rush
Sense numb
Must cum
Can't settle down

Sexual Attraction

I can't move
I can't get up
I am stuck
But I must remain still
Because I think that's the way
To control this compulsive reaction
When I think of you naked in my arms
With your hands around my waist and my ass
This is not excitement
But a deficient desire that's aching to be filled abundantly.
I can't move
I can't get up
I am stuck.

Untitled 3.6.10

Sip this potent dollar wine
Spread your legs and take this grape vine
Let it intertwine and rub all the spots
Feel it press till all the juice drops
As I grind in
And slowly pull out.
Feel the Jamaican heat.
Feel the native tongue.
Get drunk in the Jamaican wine
Squeeze your eyes tight
And beg no
From staggering with experience
And tremble with excitement.

Imagine

What do you want?
What I imagined.
So I thought I'd tease the cherry by licking the stem
slow and smooth
To give the meaning of pleasure then running
my hot tongue over your pussy
and going deeper every time I repeat;
Then slightly spreading your legs so I could run my
tongue up your belly, all over your breast, neck, in,
around, and out your ear to your soft, puffy lips, and
suck until you had no choice but to take a deep breath
as I slowly put it in, hesitatingly, to make you feel it
inch by inch and rubbing in and out, slow and smooth,
while grinding to the tempo of your smooth groove.

Inside

You feel it
I feel it
Let me know when it moves you
Let me hear the thoughts its brings you
Shout it out
Scream non stop
Let it move you
Let it bring you closer
Let it over power your senses
Making you lost to directions
Of up or down
Let it crawl below your skin
Where you cannot reach it
Let it soar above
And observe your reactions
Intently
Then
Give it back
Let it flow through you
And into me
Let the small details
Reverb astoundingly
And express in me
What is in you.

Feel Me

Let me emancipate that though that you've
been hiding about the way you feel when you see me.
Let me suck it from your lips
And squeeze it from your hips
When you look at me
And pretend there's nothing.

Let me get close
And spread your legs
And reach deep,
And release that chain that holds you afar
From exploring this body
To solidify those thoughts you've been scared to act on.

Feel me
As I feel you
Expressing your thoughts in my actions
Expressing my feeling through reactions
Feeling what you've been missing
And giving what you've been aching.

Something Juicy

Feeling the warmness of your hands in mine
Sends a tingle to my spine
that sends impulses
To my brain with this overloading sensation
that constricts
My heart to one single name
that's driving it insane
With images of us,
my dick hard, and just
short of a buss.
The image glazing at me
showing what's to be
but the sensation manifest
and my brain intensifies
The beat in my heart
that started with a sensation
that's telling me that I love you.

Rough

Every time I fuck you I want to instill pain.
I want to put my all behind it
And slam my dick in it to reach the
back to make you scream.
Your screams turn me on
And if you're not making a sound
Then I'm not doing it right.
I want you to tell me harder
And get pleasure from the pressure.
But still taking it
When your legs are on my shoulder
And when you're gripping the sheet
When I'm hitting you like that bitch doggy style
Knowing nothing feels better than coming in that pussy
That took this dick when you're pulling on me
As I push as far as I can and release

Black Light

Black light brings out the imperfections,
but there she lay, flawless.
Her body silhouette against the sheets
And her soft skin lay naked on the bed that glowed.
Her legs stretched out, and slightly apart as the light
catch the tip of her toes and carry the eyes up and up.
She's perfect because there is no blemish under the black
light that usually reveals the slightest crack in anyone.

Her skin is darker and it pulls you into the mystery
that's beneath. The mystery that's wrapped in the way
her black hair lay against an already dark skin that
makes the silhouette enticing for creating an invitation
to explore the shapes of her legs that flows to her
ass and from there to her tits, then to her face.

She sets the mood for the black light.
One that says we are alone and I'm yours to explore.
In this black light you must use the sense of touch to
fill in the dark shadow cast on her skin by the light
that your eyes cannot define. The kind of touch that
draws an image in the brain, which removes a piece
of the puzzle as you run your fingers over her smooth
body revealing a part of the mystery beneath.

She creates a world in this black light that requires
an attention to details. Details you cannot see. Details
that lets her know you adore her but without the use of
words. Details that illustrate that you've paid attention
and that with the feel of a touch you can find all the
right spots with your lips, finger tips, and with repeated
precision that's intended to open the mystery within.

Black Light (continued)

The black light is the gateway to her lust.
The type that keeps her eyes closed and her
body trembling with anticipation of the next
soft touch on her smooth skin that tingles her
soul and sends pleasure between her legs.
The black light is her gateway but can only be access
through the commitment to understand her mystery and
desires, and the patience required to take her away.

Perfections

Long dark haired against a smooth brown skin;
slender hips and broad on the tits with an ass like
whoa. The eyes attraction to this African Queen
with a walk that shakes her ass, with a smile that
makes you weak, and eye that puts you to sleep.
This woman with soft skin, hugs that hold you
tight, and a stature of what you desire don't
mean a thing if her mind isn't right.
She must have the intellect to keep you attuned to
her every word. She must be wise in her decisions
concerning your love for her, and you love for others.
She must respect the individual that is I Man; and be
able to express her disagreements without bias to
unrelated experiences. This woman that is perfect will
join in union my desires, my ideals, and my love with
an understanding that our imperfections is nothing
but a vessel that can never hold her less than what is
valuable on the inside. This perfection will know my
thoughts and actions, will realize my ups and downs, will
support and let me know that my ventures aren't right.
This black thong wearing with pushup bra and tank
top, this apple bottom and three inch heels dressing,
this black lipstick and pink toe nails Queen of a
Woman is my Perfection; my heart, and my soul.

Technicalities

Slide and fall into me
Let me feel you
The way your back stands up to my touch
As I run my fingers from your neck to your butt.
Then look into your eyes as I reach that spot
At the bottom of your back
And rub it so lightly
With care
Feeling
Desire
To stare in your eyes
Pull you closer
And kiss
Squeeze
Firmly
And suck
Licking
Wanting
To feel the next level
The passion
Of unification
Of one soul to another
Eternal
A moment that's full
Over flowing
Sweet

Untitled 3

Smooth and sensual was the breath and sounds
That glowed and vibrated through your body.
Hot was the passion burning between your legs
and deep was the tongue from my mouth.
Hard were your nipples that begged to be licked,
and hard was my dick anticipating that good clit.
Nice and smooth was the tongue as it licked you out,
and rough and deeper it got to make you shout.
Staring at you with that bullish instinct, and using my
hand, tongue, and dick to interpret what you think.
Given power I did not want to lose, so I turned you on,
low, and long, until time for me to get on; transforming the
cool, the hot, the passion, the sounds, and the vibration
into monolithic affirmation of this night's destination.
Putting out the heat when my dick and your pussy meets.
Pushing off the bed so my dick reach deep as you try to
keep quiet with pleasure as you gripped my back and leave
marks to show the measure of it running again and again.
Holding me still to enjoy the feeling, holding me
tight so it stays just right, holding me so you could
twist and moan to make the vibes last a moment.
Laying there in full physical pleasure

Nightmares

Haunted by your touch
That drags through my mind
One finger at a time
Of you laying them over my face
And running down my chest
With a very slow
Purpose
To tease my manhood
With anticipation of your love
As reality is a dream
Waiting for my eyes to close
For the fantasy of rapid eye movements
At the beauty in your eyes
Lips
Breast

Ass
Pussy
Legs
And touch;
To never be waken
To never be without
Your presence
Your smell
Of your hair
Your taste
Of your lips
Your comfort
Of being inside you
And never to be awaken
To a nightmare of being
Without you

Chapter 2

Love

Love's Beginning

I don't know love. I've never been taught to love.
I've been taught wrong and right and recognize it
before I have to find out the hard way;
and this is what I apply to love.
If it feels good then there must be love;
even if some bad exist.
And I accept it as is because we've been
told that love conquers all.
I've been told, "I love you" and never return the favor.
I've been begged to say it, but would just turn over.
I don't know love.
I've walked over hearts with a record book on
the side adding notches after notches.
If you can't tell me you love me,
then you can't be with me;
and even when you do, things didn't change.
I don't recognize your love.
Now I'm experiencing love's beginning.
Now I'm experience the pain that goes with being alone
when the person you want won't answer your calls,
now I'm having sleepless nights because
that person don't care to see me anymore.
Now I'm crying because I know how to love,
and now I'm taking my experience to make sure
that I never love wrong;
again.

Fallen Angel

I gaze with amazement of the possibilities
Not knowing which way to go
But knowing this is a moment
And a choice that will define the future
One that's eagerly anticipated
With certainty that leaves confusion
With an un-assurance of faith
Tangled within a need replaced by beauty
A secret greed to capture
You
And lay out every
Thought
That knows its desire
To treat you childlike
With protective love
And caring guidance to
Lay a foundation
Of you and me
That no one can separate.
I'm an angel
Sent for you
And each moment is creation
Something
For ever new

Lost in your love

Don't know where it's taking me
and don't care where it's going
as long as we go together.

Lost in the rapture of your beauty
and don't want to be found.
Don't want to lose the way your eyes glaze over
when I stare at you for hours.

Lost in your kiss
and I still can't tell which way is up or down
after it has ended;
and can only remember feeling like the things that makes
the stars shine at night
when I lick the juice from my lips after that kiss.

I don't want to be found.
I don't want to wake up and realize this is a dream.
I want to stay lost in your love;
not knowing what time it is,
or how many hours have passed us by
when we spend those moments together laughing,
teasing,
and playing.

Submissive

I give in like a sand trap
You suck me in and it's hard to escape this path.
You engulf me
From head, to heart, to toe.
You think,
And there I go,
Knowing exactly what to do,
And all cause,
I want you;
So bad,
It's sad,
So desperately,
So not ambiguously,
so open,
Like the window to space
Like the keys to a new place
Like the river ending to the sea;

I'm submissive
To your desire,
Wants,
Needs,
Pleads
Submissive as water in a cup
That you'll drink up,
To quench your thirst
As first
As day's light
As it shines bright
To produce a blinding sight,
And I'm submissive,
Carelessly,
Eternally.

Inadequate

I put you on a pedestal because I love you.
I can over look your flaws because we all have them.
My focus is the end result
and is doing whatever it takes to achieve it.

Standing in the back ground
while you do your things that makes you happy
and I do it with a smile.

I make sure the tools you need are in abundant
and that you'll never need.

If there's a disagreement
then it's automatic that I'm to blame
because that's not as important as seeing your smile.

I let you sleep for days without a touch
and forgive every action of misunderstandings
with a prophetic apology because I put you first,
and will do anything this love requires to keep you
on that pedestal.

The Other Lover

It's sad to see you kiss
because I'm the man on the side.
Sad to see the way you smile
Because it's not the same smile for me
Your stare is paralyzing
But only to our possibility of love
I'm the other lover,
And it's a sad affair.
We do everything you do with him
But I'm only second to his kiss, smile, and love
I'm only second but not for long
Because the attraction that pulls you to me,
And the desire that holds you keeps growing,
But it's sad,
The time in between when your eyes,
Mind and heart decide I'm no longer the other lover,
But your man

Not Me

I am not him
and even if similar he is not within
His outlook it tunneled
And my vision is balanced.

I am not him but within
There are similarities in every man
we all have desires and sin
but separate by our foundation.

I am him and he is me
wanting to be with you
lusting for your body
and having known you.

But now he is gone
and I am here
Time to move along
and let go of your fear.

My foundation is strong
my views is balanced
my desire have been long
And my commitment is sealed.

I Need Love

its not good enough that you're with me.
I'm a woman that has desires that needs to be met.
I am female that will grow into a lady
with the correct stimulus.
I do for you and you appreciate it by us being together.
I'll do anything you ask, out of love;
and I'll without you asking.
But if you can't see, then I'll tell you,
I need love.
It's more than a kiss on the cheek;
it's more than a text message a day.
Not only do I need to hear it but I need to feel it.
I need love.
I need you to show me in your movement
when you kiss me in the morning.
I need it to feel sweet when you text me that you miss me.
I'm growing, and changing, and I need you to keep up.
I am a woman and I need a woman's love.
I need you to hold me tight,
squeeze me right,
and slap me on the ass just to know you still love it.
I need your eyes on me, your hands strength to hold,
and your hot breath to keep me warm on those nights.
I'm needy of love, and I need your love.

Walk Away

What do you do when love walks away?
Do you let it go and hope the cliché is true,
or do you chase after it and hope not to look like a fool?
Do you respect the decision that its over
even if it doesn't feel that way,
or do you pursue to convince it should be another way?
What do you do when love is walking away?
How do you stop something that's already set in motion?
How can one jump out of love and leave you loving alone?
Love never leaves, people do;
and we are imperfect,
and when we can't handle love;
that's what we do.

Love Cycle

It's been long, waiting for your voice to say hello,
I miss you. Desire is cheap and I'm drunk with anticipation
when those miss you turns into a kiss. The cycle is in
rotation and it's too late to stop the flow of particles
with my love. So the heart pumps and my body is in
overdrive, waiting, idling, and imagining the rush of my
scent to your cells and your reaction to this mechanism.
This machine takes a connection to start from that
spark that ignites when my eyes see your beautiful
face, curvy body, and long flowing black hair.
The pedals begins to rotate as we step towards each
other anticipating that connection that wraps your waist
and pull you closer, that looks in your eyes and approach
with a steady amazement, and a kiss on soft lips with the
feeling of unlocking the perfect combination. Lets ride
this natural occurrence, lets swim in enticements, going
to and from with motions up and down when I lick my lips
after we kiss, begging for more, and sucking every taste
of you from my wet lips; then coming in to take more;
More of this juice that drives my cells high and
charged from this liquor that staggers me with your
love, and this thing that drives me to please you.
This is my Love Cycle; it needs your touch to start
and your love to operate. To keep it going you do
what you have to. You sneak out, you lie, and you
stay out late, just so you can preserve this chemistry
that moves us closer and closer. This full of body, aim
with target locked on, this sway between connections
that work in symmetry, that cuddles when needed,
that tickles the right spot, this Love Cycle.

Help

I lost myself in you
And I was begging to be found,
But instead,
I was doomed
Like a killer on lock down.
This spark created hope,
But sometimes it's just smoke.
The fire never grew,
And you really never knew,
How I felt,
And the limits I'd go
To prove more than you know.
But I was lost in you,
Couldn't find a way out,
No matter how we argued,
No matter how much we shout.
In a daze of your love,
I grew weary to combat
And I am still lost in a love
That I don't want to be found,
Cause I'd rather be with you,
Than to be left alone.

12.27.02 11:30 p.m.
Revised 2.2.03 11:11 a.m.

Today I called for love
And I heard a gently purr
I felt faithfully giving to love
But inside feeling empty with
Sorrow lingering on my brow
and tear drops falling down my face
and wondering if true love will
answer with her name

Drop

Drips from the luminescence of the moon
Runs wild through her veins
That beat rapidly.
Touched by the flow of the stars
Hence her sense of self is far greater than anyone's reach.
No matter how much you think you add up
It's still not enough to captivate this Goddess
Sent from the universe that bears her life.
An eclipse cannot darken her spark
And your hate cannot remove her drive.
She is woman
Given from above
Create to be one, and all
And all in one.
She's a drop from the heaven
From a cloud of rain
Following a thunderstorm.
She is woman, she is earth.
She gives birth, she feeds,
She knows how to satisfy every need
From the babe to the man and back to the woman
She is perfection
She is woman

Cruel Heaven

Heaven is cruel,
Because it didn't explain our love
Heaven can wait,
Because I want this love
Heaven gave me a taste,
And I didn't understand,
And heaven gave my emotions meaning,
My heart reason,
To beat,
To race,
To live
Give me back heaven,
Don't be so mean.
Give me back reason,
To enjoy this earth
Heaven can wait,
And heaven will always be there;
But if this is just a taste,
Then I don't want to waste time
To get to heaven
Heaven knows I'm not patient,
And it's driving me crazy,
Waiting for another piece
Give me heaven,
Bring her back in my arms.
Give me understanding,
So that heaven will never leave,
Take a break,
Or sleep.
Give me heaven,
Give me piece.

Drunk

You can't sleep,
No matter how dark your room is the middle of the day.
You can't eat because you feel nothing on the inside
and nothing can full that emptiness.
You close yourself away from the world
in your isolated pockets of your brain
behind your shut door that stays closed for days.
You don't want to move,
just lay there as lifeless as possible
because your heart is broken.

Feel

I lost feelings, emotions,
and cares.
I want to love. I want to be loved.
I want to experience the pure joy
of living for another,
And of not caring.
I've been closed,
and I must let this go.
I must feel. I must feel.
Give me hope,
Give me love.
Give me you
Let me get lost in your love
I want emotional security from your praise
I want to know you'll be there for me
I don't want to worry
To consider
To wonder

Where you stand
I want to know it
And never question it.
I want to feel.
I want to get rid of this loneliness
That I was borne as such
I want commitment
I want to give
My all
To love
To feel,
Wanted.
I want to feel my emotions.
I want your love.
I need it

Plan B

Love,
Hurt,
Misunderstandings,
Happiness.
Shut me in your love,
Hide me in your bosom,
Give me love unconditionally,
Give me all of you,
Each of your beautiful long black curly hair,
Your soft tiny lips,
Your sweet tasty slender neck,
And all your love
Give me your small hips,
Your fat ass,
Your long legs,
Your big pussy;

And your love
Give me your all,
Give me your pain,
Make me your desire,
Give me your hand to hold,
Give me your eyes to see,
Give me your brain to teach,
Give me your heart to love,
Give me your love;
And I'll give you my world,
And I'll make you my heaven,
And I'll give you all of me,
And I'll make love forgotten,
And I'll make us love,
And I'll make us one.

So What

Why should I have to go through this pain alone?
If you have to hurt too then I'll be good with that.
I want to know it makes you moan
At night before you sleep.
Leaves you feeling empty in the mornings
When you feel for me and there's nothing but space.
Getting lonely,
Cause I'm not there to share a story.
If your hurt makes your knees buckle
And your legs fear walking then I'm just as happy.
So what,
I don't want you to be in a better place,
I want your mascara to race down your face,
I want there to be no relief from the ache in your stomach,
I want to see you cringe at night dying to sleep,
But cannot,
So what,

We were not meant to be,
But I can't go through this alone
Cause we started this together,
And that's how we should end it,
You feeling the pain you brought,
The confusion from your silence,
The loneliness from you not being there for me,
Feel the hurt,
And beg to let it go away,
And then I'll smile
If you come crawling back,
And enjoy your pain,
And I'll be happy,
So what.

Crash

When love goes head to head at full speed
And someone leave a trail of steel,
of red that was bled,
From emotions that were shed,
In hopes to achieve,
The heart's desire and dream;
With one left standing
And wondering.
With an impact so great,
That it turns your faith,
From loving
To hating,
From wanting
To pushing,
From needing,
To forgetting.
Love has crash and its burning
and there's no one to put out the flame
and now this love is piercing
and you think it was just a game.
And love continue to burn
And you don't know why
when you sleep you toss and turn
and sometimes cry.
Love at full speed
and now it must stop
Love at full speed
now it's a death trap.

Love's Dying

We hurt each other effortlessly.
Where is love?
Has love changed, or has it devolve?
Love in me is strong,
as my desires are for purity, passion, and purpose,
but why does my love seems flat lined?
Your love for me is new,
and better than your many loves before.
Its unique in its mystery of how it got started,
how high it climbed with each kiss,
and to avail to this sentiment of lack of trust.
Where is that seed that was planted
that tells you when you find perfection
that should blossom in to the most beautiful flower?
Love is dying.
Slowly it drips,
and drains,
and without tears.
Love is flat lining and we need to believe,
in Love.

Walk Away

What do you do when love walks away?
Do you let it go and hope the cliché is true,
or do you chase after it and hope not to look like a fool?
Do you respect the decision that its over
even if it doesn't feel that way,
or do you pursue to convince it should be another way?
What do you do when love is walking away?
How do you stop something that's already set in motion?
How can one jump out of love and leave you loving alone?
Love never leaves, people do;
and we are imperfect,
and when we can't handle love;
that's what we do.

Love Simple

So, your love will never die.
It remains the top of your love experience.
The kind that is woken with a simple text
asking how's your day.
Getting to this height was not easy,
but we all sacrifice for love,
and yours was difficult cause you thought you
would never love again; yet,
still you fall at the sound of his voice,
and you can't refuse an invite to spend the night,
because this love will never die even though it keep you up,
sometimes crying and trying to figure out why can't
love be simple.

Pillow Love

Left alone,
Crying for days,
Crawling out of bed,
And then back in.
Holding the pillow tight,
Squeezing it to give meaning,
And to release this pain
Not eating,
And not giving in,
Not caring
But still deeply in love,
Understanding denial
But still not giving up hope
Staying awake
In deep dream,
In a trance
With a pillow between your legs,
And one under your eye,
To catch the tears,
Still looking for understanding,
And a reason to move on;
And a reason why,
A reason for self healing,
And giving your pillow love,
Time,
Dreams,
And that commitment
You're not getting.

Humbled

I've got a swag that's attractable.
I hold myself at a very high esteem.
I know I have a big ego,
and a confidence that's unimaginable.
And,
there you are,
Perfect.
You bring my heart to a standstill
with your presence.
Your aura changes my existence
of what it was to what it could be,
and will be.
You've changed my walk,
my talk,
and my emotions to reflect obedience through faith,
that we are bound like stars in the sky,
and oceans to this earth.
No longer is anything important to being with you,
and now I'm humbled for this present
from God,
with love that is pure,
and true.

As if it wasn't there

Love ended
I think of the good times and smile.
I think of the bad times and frown.
I think of where love could've gone,
And I think about where it's been.
We spent countless hours doing
everything that brings love to great heights,
And then tore it down in one night.
There are no regrets, and no remorse;
And love is buried and gone;
As if it wasn't there.

Chapter 3

Life

Garden

I'll make some good ones and some bad ones,
and then I'll put some in the middle.
Ha-ha, what a funny combination.
Let's make it a little more interesting.
We'll make everything perfect then tempt
them with something better.
If they fall for it then let's give them rules to follow,
and hardships to bear.
If they follow our first instruction
then let's leave them happy.

Is that cruel or blind justice?

It's my strings to pull so does it even matter
how it looks or how they feel?
What else can I do?
I'm not bored but let's see what options they'll choose,
self gratification or enlightenment?

Let's not change the mixture, good, bad, and in between.
Self motivated, dependent, or don't care either way.
What excitement, rise and fall.

Grace

To walk in his footstep
To forgive
Knowing that the outcome
Is not desired
And doing the right thing
How can we not be happy
Knowing that His grace has endured
Our actions
And that we must
Copy his results
To truly
Accept faith's hand,
And only by grace
Can we come closer
And by grace
We shall move on,
Living full,
Free,
Lovingly,
For all his creation,
And by grace
For our soul's emancipation

Natural

Small inset with everything needed
It's beautiful, and perfectly drafted.
Every item place, every options considered,
Every color imaginable.
Every though picked to ensure success is beyond ample.
Still, it's not natural.
It cannot be duplicated.
Nature's intent to be free and not harvested.
Nature changes within cycles to ensure longevity,
Unity, and uncongested.
It is beauty, but unmaintained it loses its naturality,
And nature takes care of itself.

Untitled 7

Creation through imagination
relaxes the temporal extensions
Leaving the road wide open to run free
Feel the wind
Take a breath
Lie on the grass and imagine death
Not fearing
Realizing
Accepting
Laughing
Playing with the thunder and mysterious wonders
Mentally getting younger

Guidance

Collectively pulling together
Climbing on each other,
Creating an existence
That leaves a trail of guidance.
Slowly and surely,
Moving steadily,
Leaving trails to follow
Pulling deep within
To overcome any selfish feeling,
Knowing that it's eminent,
That everything done in the present,
Will reflect brightly on future circumstance
The path was never easy,
But each step closer is pleasing.
Collectively building,
Pulling and stacking,
Creating a positive future
For all children

Man

Self taught, self love, self raised, selfish.
Guidance, lack of,
woman to be your route to man hood.
Confusion, blinded love
Acceptance at a glance, rejection follows.
Denial, no other option
Self adjust, lost uniqueness,
Path clouded, aim misdirected.
Hope reaches, commitment follows.
Happiness momentarily, man's reality constructed.
Hatred and lust, self pleasing and don't give a fuck.
Goals disappear, hope slipping.
Faith reassure, love's giving.
Rebuild, up, push, life
Forgive self, sleep.

Missing

What is it that you like to do,
Run through girls, maybe I'll do that too,
But ten babies, I think not, maybe.
I'm your only son that's seeking affection
Even though I'm a man,
And not a terrible one
There's still something missing
Part of the plan
And that I'm still seeking
To make me understand,
To make me feel whole.
It's something you think you can't do without
But something you need
To feel complete.

Follow me

You are in me
And everything I do
You should follow me.
I've been there
And that's why I'm taking the lead
Follow me.
I watched you grow,
So I know your smile
And your likes
So follow me
Cause I know you.
Trust my words
Cause they are spoken out of care.
Trust my directions,
Cause I have experience,
Trust in me,
Because I'm living for you,
So follow me,
So I can be proud of you
And help you
To be who you want to be;
And if I'm lucky,
You will choose me.

Cat

A smile as grizzly as death
And beauty that makes a cop sweat
This is her
Smart beyond her years
And confident among her peers
Forever searching for answers
With challenge to every doubt
And conscious of the moment
And react with positive affirmation.
A tool that will slice fear in two
But an angel with suspenseful love for you
Do not debate your thoughts for her
Kindly discuss
And don't take her for a fool
Else you'll realize her confident
Angelic
Double edged tool.

Corporate Ladder

He climbs, makes his way to the top
but through loops holes and sits there hoping to not be
discovered. As he perch and loses time; wiser but none the
better; he learns the ins and outs. He gets educated first
hand, and uses this glorified experience to please himself.

He plays the game, losing time; he plays the game,
loosing self; he plays the games with smiles and assurance
that he will remain on top; and never
think twice about looking down.

Now wiser to the short rope he created;
he struggles to balance morals with opportunity.
He fights but it's too late, he's engulfed in timeless
behavior. And he struggles to reveal true identity.

I must cry

Weakness is never an option,
And burdens must be carried with a smile.
Man is strength.

Knowledge profound;
And with the correct answer every time.
Man is friendship

Family maintained;
Providing food, guidance, and love.
Man is commitment.

But, achieving isn't easy,
And the path taken to secure manhood
Is dug with secrets and hidden pain;
And the burdens we carry from appearing to be strong
To the secrets we keep even when it's wrong,
And changing to make that commitment and deny self
Are rooted deep within
and we must sometimes let it show
That even as a man,
it's not a contradiction that sometimes
I must cry.

I Want Love

I want love. I don't want to imagine what it feels like.
I want to experience love and know that it is.
My past could not have been love
because they are not even in my present.
The emotions I feel could not have been love
because I imagine I would know that it is
and I knew that it wasn't.
Deep down I feel wronged in my approach and reproaches,
but still feel abundantly satisfied that I was honest
with giving it my all to no end with love.
I want it.
Did I let it go because I didn't know love?
I truly don't think so.
Can I ask for less and think it is love, definitely not.
I know I haven't experienced love,
even if it's my fault, imagination, or others selfish,
manipulative desires that blocked the chances
to let my heart be free to explore the vast
emotional, physical, and spiritual connection
that unifies two beings into one
without the need to question the little things
but to accept the obvious.
I want love.
I want you.

Real

Love is not impartial
It's sustaining.
It's never taking your eyes off the prize,
The one thing that's important
That makes you whole,
Agile,
Precious,
Vicious,
And patient
Love has no limits
But understands that a battle is not the end,
That tears are new beginning of a journey
Down a new road but to the same goal,
Sustained by commitment,
And impartial to anything that does not define
Your reason,
To live

Gateway

Pupils are white
But sadness within
Darkened gateway to the soul
Of terrible feelings
Smile is bright
But a tongue lay silent
To protect love
And keep the pain within
Beautiful face
Becomes the façade
Hiding that smile
That keeps everything shut within.
And saddened are the eyes
Unable to sleep
Seeing images
Awake and asleep
Keeping memory
And taunting dreams
Eyes of sadness
Behind a beautiful smile
Covered in memory
Lost in time

A Rose

Asked a rose petal floating on the wind
Where have you been?
Were you deeply rooted
In enriched soil that supported all your needs
To grow from a stem to a beautiful flower,
And were you picked by young lady in love
Or a carefully pruning gardener?
Are you an I love me or love me not?
Or a secret gift of what another feels
For another,
Tell me,
Where have you been?
How did you get here?
Laying gently in my hand
Teasing my emotions
Of your life span
From gazing at your color
And curves,
Wanting to know how they got there,
And what you've seen;
But left to wonder,
How you made it from the earth
Into my hand

Jewel

Dangling by a rose from strings concocted of silk
reshaping the harsh rays of the sun
in reflections of hypothalamus engagements,
lip enticements,
air of a dove's wing with the melancholy of an African
waterfall against the sweet melodious music
of a harp and soft love songs by Marvin Gay,
thinking, waiting for the privilege to construct
on what should be cherished,
treasured, and giving nothing less than pure love.

Winter Wonders

Beautifully falling chaos pattern of unique symmetry
creating haze of blinding sight,
leaving the black to white
and the dirty to pure.
Creating a wanting to be held,
and finger tips to be warmed.
Slowly it builds and decreases,
getting artistic but dramatic.
Adding beauty on beauty
layers on layers.
It hardens, and hurts, and locks you in.
It forces you to remain still,
until it lets go and melts,
dripping beauty like wet mascara,
creating a black,
dirty slush that's washed down the drain.

Conrod Thomas

Mouse Trap

My journey is complete.
It was to put you in a place
Where you lie, and cheat.
I broke your heart
Without regard,
But you broke mine too,
And it puts us apart.
Sorry,
I can't be friends,
This road has hit a dead end.
My job was to break you
Like I always do,
Cause my purpose
Is to break hearts,
But yours was set apart from the rest,
Cause you truly were the best,
I've ever had,
But taming you was a hard part of the plan,
And now you're prepared to move on.
I don't regret a day,
Except for the first,
When seeing you created a thirst,
One that had to be quenched,
And now I've drank my gull full,
And you got to go,
So good by fool
But don't forget,
The experience made you better than before,
And now you won't cheat any more.

No reflection

I stare and I see no reflection of me.
There I look,
and it's like an empty book.
I recognize the shape
But no details to share my faith.
I look deeper
And it gets creepier;
No brows, no smiles,
Not scowls, no eyes.
Still I search,
Staring inside,
Removing all the bondage to see
What beneath lies.
And so goes the layers,
And pieces of me appears,
And with thought I construct what isn't there,
And still I don't see a reflection of me,
But what I will be.

Hurt

There are no rules to this relationship, but we like
each other, and grew very fond of our time together.
Now you're gone. It may be for a short while
compared to our time on earth, but it still hurt.
The pain of our misunderstandings starting with this
young beginning is overshadowing our short time spent
together overcoming the hurt of past relationships. Let
truths be told of our feelings without the worry that
giving full access to our emotions will bring hurt. Let
understanding and acceptance of circumstance belittle
any idea that those situations may bring unwanted hurt
even though time together is so sweet, as compared to
the first kiss. Let the hurt subside for the days and nights
we shared in each other's warmth from me hugging your
naked body as we lay side by side and kiss. Let the hurt
subside cause we went there and enjoyed every hump
along the path but never deterred from the feeling that
enforce the reasons why you do not wish to be hurt.
Trust is not the issue, cause the youth of enjoyment from
talking, and learning the little things adds up to the great
feelings of wanting and understanding each other's likes;
and having no trust cannot bring hurt cause it's so new.
Let go of the hurt and enjoy the memories that's created.
Keep the hurt a dew with the anticipation of seeing and
achieving that feeling that makes you relax because
your eyes are happy to know that we made it into each
other's arms. Let go of the hurt and release the pain
that the heart does not desire and the mind's restless
pursuit of explanations over and over and over again.

Lap Dogs

So they roam from home to home
spreading seeds to anyone willing
to open up lying down
because the lingua is so sweet
from failed experiments
to the next as pre-programmed
to do one,
thing,
only,
fuck.

The Moment

Greatness is not given, it's taken.
You know when it's that time to be great.
You feel it and it's like nothing else.
The path is clear and the choice is easy.
Regardless of the plot to achieve it,
Once you decide to be great,
Nothing else will get in your way.
You grasp that moment, swallow,
And choose to grab it.
Run with it.
Live it.
Be it.
Greatness is perpetual, duplicated,
And never exaggerated

Change

Living to the fullest
Creation at its best
Moving up the ladder
Leaving all the rest
Knowing the destination
And how to achieve it
Planning the future
And believing it
Change
Staying on the path
At a pace
That leaves room to enjoy
The journey
Slowing down to observe
That it's not a race

I Can

Dream,
Reach out,
Feel it,
Grab it.
Attainable is hope
When pursued immensely
For a solution from that viable path
Take leaps
Not steps
Go above
And beyond
And accept no imitation.
Do not hold back
Or hold it in
You know from that feeling
You know from desire
You know life
Dreams,
Faith
And the pursuit
Of happiness
Is within
Reach.

Ghetto

We cling to the little things
and you wonder why we fuss so much
it's because the little things
means so much
cause that's all we have
and we don't see getting much
no matter how hard we try
because of our area code
and other codes
and quotas
set by elements of society
that's past down generations
to generations
with no one
with the learning
to break the code
cause we've been stuck
in the ghetto.

Footsteps

Paranoia runs deep
Trying to figure where to go from day to day
Asking, what makes me a man?
Trying to figure out how to take control
How to let my swagger roll
How to be
All I can be
And
Still
Please
You
But it's not that easy
Cause I never knew
From a lesson or a talk
How to act or walk
And it's something I got to figure out
Sometimes through screams and shouts
While I strive to be a better man

For
You
To show you something great
But time has past
And it seems
Too late
And even though there's hate
Lurking beneath
And trying not to walk in your feet
It's still hard
To not
Be
Just
Like
You

Hit

Pass the food
The element to let time stand still
Lean back and inhale
Draw in the street
The misguided future attempts to
enjoy the last days of freedom
A dissolute,
Isolation on one rock
And exhale fear
None left within
Reality bites
It feeds the ego that human addiction
To accomplish all achievements
Exhale fear
Attempts tried
Steps gained
It's grimy
It's fucked
There's no fear
Suicide kings

Culture

How can you resist this beauty of the streets?
A pearl polished and dignified,
The culture coming back,
Force to action with desire for fame,
And recognition
The life,
Loving enough to seek new avenues,
To test faith with courage, packing,
And faith to fight daily
This love of creation and to new beginnings
Explorers with a drive for change, dreams, life
Welcome back to the streets.

Dangerous Element

There they sit
The usual suspects
Air filled with purple haze
And stares at your things
It's the heart of the city
They bring back to this community
The grit of the underground
Old school
Old Heads
Dangerous elements
Old fool with high temperament.
Each minute heightened till the next
Ready at every moment for life's end
And filled with laughter of days stories and
Gambling but keeping one eyes looking left
And the other looking right
Living for the moment as dangerous elements

Playing in the streets

Desperate by desire
A wild card dealt that's me
Fitting of my britches
Cause I've backed it up
But to what avail.
Stubborn and bad,
A rebel,
Born in the streets.
In search of heritage
A game we play
With balls to climb.
Me.
Ego comes secondary,
Pride will kill,
Kind of brother
Back in the streets
Slums
Back alley life.
Future dreams,
Stardom now,
Me.

Getting High

To dream and fly
A paradigm of getting high
No more fights
Just mental drive while I'm feeling high
To take a puff and blow
To inhale and hold
To watch time slow down
To ease back and lay down
No troubles or pain around
Just puffing my weed and watch the ash fall to the ground

Part II

It's time to do what I feel
Conquer the world in a day
Stop work and make everyone play
Fly to the moon on sheer will power
Stop all clocks at half pass the hour
You say how can I?
And I say has anyone proved I cannot?
Let's prove it and never stop
Let's make fun while on top
Let imaginations soar and hearts dream
Let's feel free as human beings.

Blah

I don't feel very bright
With the circumstance of my current plight
I'm stable and true
but my feelings are misguided and blue.

I think I'm smart,
But I don't know what to do,
I think with my heart
And I steel feel stuck like glue.

I don't know if I should re-start
Or how this journey will go,
And not knowing how to let go,
Keeps this angry flow.

I wish and I pray
For a better day,
But still I roam as if I lost my way
Thinking of when I can relax and play.

I'm stuck in my plight
With no change in sight
I still love me for me
But wish to be free

Breadth

It's so warm.
I get just what I need
and I'm never without.
Some times a little shaky but never too rough
I sit here waiting for the right time
till my craw is full
and it's time TO LET GO and get out.
I don't need to stay here too long.
I must find my own digestions.
I must start the next step in evolution.
So I go with instinct and I push,
I claw, I peck, I do what is needed to get an opening
to work with.
I study the surroundings,
get in a comfortable spot and work from that spot.
It cracks but not break; relief, I can breathe.
I continue the pursuit for the natural feeling from within
and with every breath I take
and every kick I make
my breaths become shorter,
and shorter
And I must get out.

A new day

Beginning in a continuous cycle
That's giving a chance each day
With hopes that lessons learnt
Are not repeated
And even when done so,
There is still room for hope
With a new day.
A circle that stays constant
With outcomes
But reduces
With the inability to recognize
That a new day
Brings new hope
And hope
Garner change
For another new day

Still

Stand still and fall so I can catch you
and create that trust your heart will never forget.
Stand against the wall and spread them
so I can search your body
and leave it begging to be abused.
Stay still while I adore your curves
and imagine how it got sculpted.
Stay still and let time catalyze
this precious moment for an eternity.
Don't move while I approach you with delight
moving towards you slowly.
Don't move until it feels just right
when your eyes behold my feelings.
Rest your fears on my shoulder
for me to carry.
Rest your love in my arms
to be assured it will be there as we get older.
Lay motionless
as I explore you with touches.
Lay motionless
as I explore you with kisses.
Remember these things
and never doubt,
that these moments,
are unchanging.

Today

Window light,
Heavens bright,
Sound is sweet,
Wind beneath.

Passion boils
Temper coils
Energy release
Mind at ease

Love is pure
Great and true
Expecting favor
Happy and new

Eyes closed
Head tilted
Deep breaths
Life is gifted

Air

Death has stolen my breath away.
It crept up on me in the middle of the night
Circled above my pillow rested head
And pulled as I inhaled
Moving quickly as to keep me from waking
Death stole my breath away
But it didn't get my life.
I have millions of breaths to give death
But my life will never so easily be given
And with its attempt to suck my life
From every air pocket in my lungs
Through my nostrils whilst covering my mouth
I didn't let it be so.
My life to give is all mines to choose
And with each second gasping for air
As I'm pulled closer to death I find life.
Life to fight
Life to take it back
Life to claim it was not my time to surrender
To the reaper
And so it fled with one breath
And tried a second, and a third time in the night,
But I still had life to fight
And more breath to give to death.

Joy

Seeking joy has been a fight
It touches you on your neck
And when you turn to look
It's already out of sight
Leaving you confused
And don't know what to do
And have you following your tail like a fool.

The short instance you recognized its touch
Your emotions glowed with such a rush
Of feelings of satisfaction
And dreams of recreation

But joy is just a game
That takes two players with good aim
And when the target is not the same
Joy turns to sad complaints.

Death

In sleep it creeps up and holds me still;
toying with me and jeering at my emotions.
It paralyzes my muscles and leaves
my brain free to wonder;
but I'm not scared. I know my time will come and death
does not scare me so easily.
My purpose is being fulfilled and not even death can
circumvent it. I welcome death's challenge at every turn
and beat its challenge.
Death is nothing but a small reminder that I'm on the right
path. Life, however, is something that's a greater challenge

Predator

A new era has come, El Mastodon
Bad bull run, terror web spun
Please settle down, the end hasn't come.
What will it be, trying to flee and can't run
What will it be, trying to flee and get shot
down
How could it be, irregular fun.
Can't settle down, the end hasn't yet come
Find a place to hide, take a short breath
Now realize it's detrimental to your health.
How does it feel, the end has come.
Terror web spun
can't run
Get shot down
can't have fun
The end has come.

Army

The works of men are the testimony of Christ.
Man favors self until its destroyed,
and only then can repentance grant salvation
with a broken spirit that is necessary to stay righteous
because that heavy burden you've experienced.
Now this is not the only path
and of course righteousness from the start
is ideal,
but in case you fall,
there is still hope for the wicked,
and with an open heart for understanding
can these testaments
create soldiers
for the Lord.

Shelter

A reason to cry
To release joy or pain
Something
Anything
Needing to feel
To shed this cold exterior
To embrace reality
Love
Dreams
Hope for others.
To shed a tear
Without effort
From being in the moment
A passage that must be crossed
But now without a solution,
And a well is hidden
Beneath the precisely placed scales
That keeps it shut in
Buried,
Forever.
Begging for release.
Give me a reason to cry.

Time Piece

Moving excessively slowly
Along the manicured planes of my mind.
Gaining speed at each inch,
And still not going anywhere.
Thoughts drifts lifelessly in and out of reality,
Leaving skid marks in time,
Of services rendered as to a pinch
Of salt to make the pots flavor.
Coming and going,
Up and down,
In and out,
You and me.
Creating things adored
With precise manipulation
Designed to move emphatically free.
Free, free,
But immensely static.
So clear as a Sunday
Yet black as a Friday.
So we live,
So we play.
Moving through enigmas
Day by day.

Pull

You've sculpted a body
that's defined to express
an attraction
that's desired by the opposite sex
but your spiritual is still on its first pull up.
It's a heavy weight
that's heavier than any you'll ever lift;
and to define this spiritual muscle requires praise,
Worship,
and leadership.
This spiritual journey
needs work for it to be defined in the eyes of God,
and getting up required letting go
of that lazy feeling,
getting rid of that denial
that keeps faith abated.
This requires repetition
to be acclaimed
to reality through love,
purpose,
understanding,
fellowship,
and believing.

Pluck

Held slender with balance
Poised angled with style
Steadily strummed
And flow with resonance
Repeating with delight
Giving equations of soul
And fashioned class
Rounded with beauty
And gathering smiles
Plucking specially
With hearts guidance

Faith

Feelings unknown, unsure,
feelings cast aside,
and now must endure.
Faith denied,
future bleak,
must in God confide,
and him I must first seek.
Tomorrow may never come,
must live in the present,
adding up the sum,
of the past events.
This is a fear,
and must approach with care,
but what's for sure,
I know I need faith to get me there.

One

What is this curled up in my hand
and tugging on my finger and building
on that connection that is natural?

This symmetry of excellence and love,
that's slowly feeling the pulse rushing
through my body at her amazement.

What's this dependable element
that knows me
from the millions without seeing my face?

How is this precious little fighter
changing my outlook
to see only her future ahead of my own?

This uncontrollable factor of my life that I would die for,
clings to me for instructions on every breath;
looks at me with love in her eyes,
and gives new meaning for living.

Inspired

Grab hold and elevate
Seemingly at ease
With a grip that will hold
Till you reach that gold.
A journey that's built
One step at a time
And a vision that knows
The gold will be achieved.
A moment to never forget
A moment to drive
A moment to follow
And a moment assured.
Movement
Abound
With energy to learn
To accept failure
But not to give in
And with a smiling heart
Living
The making of a dream.